THAT'S WHAT YOU SAY

A "Thick As Thieves" Collaboration

All rights reserved. No part of this book may be reproduced or transmitted in any form or by any means without written permission from the author.

"Scripture quotations are from The ESV® Bible (The Holy Bible, English Standard Version®), copyright © 2001 by Crossway, a publishing ministry of Good News Publishers. Used by permission. All rights reserved."

THAT'S WHAT YOU SAY A "Thick As Thieves" Collaboration

Copyright © 2021 by Vanessa J White

Published By: You Can Make It Books, LLC
www.youcanmakeitbooks.com

978-1-7366651-4-5

Printed in the United States

DEDICATION PAGE

THIS BOOK IS DEDICATED TO MY MOTHER, FLORA D. JOHNSON, MY GRANDMOTHER, VIRGINIA LANIGAN, AS WELL AS MY TWO DAUGHTERS SIMONE AND MARESSA. A SPECIAL THANKS TO MY SISTERS AND BROTHERS WHO HAVE SUPPORTED AND ENCOURAGED ME OVER THE YEARS: ROSCHELL, LAMOUR, PERCY, ISSA, DENNIS, MELVIN (EVELYN), REGINALD, ROMAIN, MAKIDAH AND EVELYN.

ACKNOWLEDGEMENTS

I acknowledge my Pastor, Apostle Dr. Oscar J. Nelson, Dowdell-Underwood for his wisdom and spiritual guidance over the years, and our First Lady Dr. Helen. I acknowledge my friend Pastor Karen Staton, Vanessa Mozelle-Washington, Pastors Curtis and Ann White, Dr. Maxine Miller and my late husband, Bishop Jesse White.

THANK YOU

First, I am thankful to my Lord and Savior, Jesus Christ, for keeping me through the good, and not so good, life experiences. As a result of my trials, I have developed resilience and perseverance. Next, I am thankful for my son-in-law, Jean W. Elie and his continuous prayers and praise, and for my friend, Dawn Heit, for naming this book. Thank you to Simone Elie for the design of the book cover and editing and to Maressa Emile for the collection and original publishing of these quotes, as well as, editing. To my niece, Kamilah Foster and my publisher, Leticia Starks-Underwood, who are my lighthouses in writing and publishing. My life has been improved by just being around these positive people who strive daily to make this world a better place. Thank you to all of you who have assisted me with the collection of these lessons and quotes.

Table of Content Page

PREFACE

My purpose for writing this book is to share the inspiration I have received over the years that compelled me to go forward in life. I used to think I was the only one that had major setbacks, disappointments, and thoughts of wanting to give up in life but with time I was able to overcome those obstacles. I was restored better than ever before. My goal is to share these inspirational quotes, lessons, and testimonies with the world. As I am the "sum total of all of my experiences." People have told me that I am strong, but I didn't think it was so. I remember how I felt during difficult times and how I thought that my coping skills needed to strengthen over time. I wanted to give up! I heard songs like "Let Your Power Fall by James Fortune, "(I'm a) Survivor" by Destiny's Child or The Lion King's, "I Just Can't Wait To be King" and knew I was not the only one. There had been times when I placed inspirational quotes and scriptures on my bathroom mirror and rehearsed them daily, but I did not see the manifestation until I began to be grateful. Now, I can look back over my life and see where I came from.

I was born in the cellar of my mother's home, delivered by my grandmother. My mother was such an inspiration to me despite her seventh-grade education. She said many of the quotes included in this book. The most prominent quote that comes to mind is, “I could write a book,” but she never did. I now know the strength it took for her to raise myself and my ten siblings. Some years ago, my pastor, Dr. Oscar J. Nelson, Dowdell-Underwood, prayed over me and announced that I would write many books and now I am writing my first. His most recent publications entitled, “I am Possible” are inspiring words that spoke directly to me. Despite the negativity of the world, I found the words and a state of mind to remain positive. These words became a part of my daughters' vocabulary. I would hear them speak and they were saying my words like it was second nature. They would say things like, “That’s what you say, Mom." Recently, they gave me a photograph of them together and it included the caption, “Mom, we get it now.” I smiled as I hung the picture in my living room. I knew they had profited from my words and just maybe you can too.

"WHEN OTHERS RAN OUT, HE RAN IN…" #1

Face your fears.

I had a serious phobia of blood and needles. If I had an appointment to have blood drawn for labs, I would have an anxiety attack and felt like I would pass out. I wanted to overcome the fear but did not know how.

I prayed and shortly afterwards I passed a billboard on Highway 930. The background showed a picture of the Twin Towers burning on 9/11. In the foreground was a firefighter running toward the towers with soot on his face, wearing an oxygen tank on his back. The caption read, "When others ran out, he ran in." I said, "I want to be like that." Soon after, I registered for a 16-week phlebotomy class. If the teacher was lecturing, I was fine but as soon as she told us to break into groups and start drawing blood on each other, I had to go outside and stand in the snow without a coat on. As the weeks progressed and the weather warmed up, it was not enough for me to stand outside. I would then go into the restroom, splash water on my face and put my head down between my knees. I finally finished the class but I was still nervous. On the last day of class, I had eight people to practice drawing my blood and I had successfully completed my 100 sticks. As I left the room, a classmate came over to me and asked if she could draw my blood. I explained that I had been drawn eight times. She replied, “I need two more sticks to pass the class,” so I agreed and said “Don’t go in a hole that's already made...” This was the second time in my life that I had to face my fears.

"KEEP GETTING UP & GOING TO BED" #2

Experience is the best teacher.

This quote is especially useful to young teens who are just starting to experience life. Many times, they think they know more than their parents. Just keep living and you will hopefully, understand how life and the world operates. If we choose to operate under the assumption that everything is "rosy" or that the world is evil then everything is a matter of black and white and there are no shades of gray. What is life but the sum of all of our experiences? We will have good days and not so good days, but we are survivors. Maturity and wisdom are a life-long process. Just keep living!

"EVERY CLOSED EYE AIN'T SLEEP AND EVERY GOODBYE AIN'T GONE" #3

People are listening when you think they're not.

Funny story: My mother lived with us in her last days of life, after being diagnosed with Alzheimer's. Each day her home health aide came to assist her with grooming and hygiene, and she would tell the home health aide whatever was going on in the household. I spoke with mom and explained that whatever happened in the home wasn't anyone else's business. It did not matter what it was, she just wanted to tell something. Her bedroom shared a wall with my room and one evening, my daughter Maressa knocked on my bedroom door and reported that "Big Mama" was listening to my phone conversation. So, I turned on the weather channel on the television. The next day when the home health aide arrived and asked her how she was doing, my mother said, "Partly cloudy, chance of rain."

“GOD ROVIDER” #4

"God will never leave you or forsake you."

Several years ago, I was informed by my Department Chair that everyone at the university who did not have a master’s degree would be discharged due to accreditation guidelines. “But you are safe,” she told me. At that moment I heard the voice of God say, “I am your provider.” Months later the college closed suddenly. However, I had been offered a Department Chair position at another university within weeks of that conversation. I did not know what "provider" meant until I started that new job at the age of 62. I prayed and asked God what was my gift and how would He provide for me? He said, “Your gift is good health and longevity." When God gives us an opportunity, we must work the gift He has given each of us.

“THE PEN IS MIGHTIER THAN THE SWORD” #5
Get a Lawyer

Fighting with knives and guns will only do so much damage, but the law is stronger and more effective than arguing and physically fighting.

"PEOPLE DON'T HAVE TO BE NICE AND IF THEY ARE, THEY DON'T HAVE TO BE NICE TO YOU!" # 6

Show appreciation; be grateful.

Remember the kindness of others is their choice and not a given. Don't mistake kindness for weakness and assume that because a person is nice to you that they're obligated to show kindness to you. They could just as easily redirect their efforts to somewhere they are appreciated. Saying "thank you" makes rooms for more.

I was a supervisor at my job and there was an elderly gentleman who worked the front desk security. I overheard other employees talking about how prejudice he was, although I had never heard him say anything inappropriate until the day I arrived for the second shift after working my day job. He pushed the security button to unlock the door and I proceeded past him. I threw my hand up to wave "hello", as I passed his desk. He said "Black people are always late…", I kept walking. A few days later he was observed asleep at his post and I was summoned to write him up. I asked him to step in the hallway and while making eye contact with him I explained that he was in danger of losing his job. I asked if there was anything I could do to help him. I offered gum and suggested he drink water or stand if he felt sleepy. He told me that his medication made him sleepy. So, I made a suggestion. A few days later he approached me at my desk and said he wanted to talk, so I accepted. He said, he knew that I was trying to save his job and expressed his appreciation.

“YOU WANTED TO BE GROWN, THIS IS WHAT GROWN FOLKS DO” #7

Being an adult comes with plenty of responsibilities.

This will apply to teenagers and adults with ”too much on their plate.” We can overload our schedules with activities and things that we want to do, or others may want us to do which may exhaust us. Sometimes we have to say no. I smile as my daughters, nieces and nephews take on adult responsibilities and they announce, “You made it look so easy.” Many times in life, I had to smile through tears until the storm had passed. Now we give each other a “high five” and laugh because they finally understand what it takes to be a responsible adult.

"I CAN SHOW YOU BETTER THAN I CAN TELL YOU" #8

Experience/demonstration is the best teacher.

Sometimes, we warn people of a pending outcome or ask them to stop doing a certain thing and they continue. Other times people do not believe you will do what you say. Stop talking. "Show 'em"!

"THEY ALL WENT TO THE SAME SCHOOL AND GRADUATED WITH HONORS" #9 (Flora Johnson)

It's not what they say, it's what they do.

Maya Angelou said it best, "When people show you who they are believe them." When certain characteristics are displayed by individuals you can identify which "school" of learning they embrace. They will all display certain qualities that show you who they really are. Do not be fooled when a person says what they really mean and then apologize to cover it up. Take notes and believe if a person does not keep their word, it is because that is who they are. Liars think everyone is lying and honest people may believe that others are honest because that is who they are and want to give others the benefit of the doubt.

“YOU BETTER HAVE YOUR CAB FARE HOME” #10

Always have a backup plan.

Whenever we went on a date as a young adult my mother would give us cab fare to come home. Sometimes, we can become codependent in relationships that are toxic to our well-being and we do not know how to get out of it. Mother meant for us to have a way out and to be able to stand on our own two feet. When we depend solely on another person to provide our value and security in life, we can become stagnant and unable to move, trapped, entangled or simply unable to break free. Always leave yourself a way out!

"IF YOU HAVEN'T TOLD JESUS YOU HAVEN'T TOLD ANYONE" #11

Make Jesus your confidant.

We frequently like to share our thoughts, desires and trials with our best friend. Yet sometimes we do not receive the best advice from them. You may tell your deepest secret to someone and when they get upset with you, they remind you of what you shared to hurt you and put you down. Instead, we should cast all of our cares and concerns on Jesus and have peace knowing that it's been left in His hands.

“THIS WILL BE A GOOD EXPERIENCE FOR YOU” #12

Each choice manages its own consequence

When a person does not heed advice, do not agonize over it. Allow them to grow in their decision to walk in chaos. Be positive, be strong and standby in faith on their behalf.

"MAJORING IN MINOR THINGS" #13

Don't sweat the small stuff.

Choose your battles carefully. Sometimes we focus on the minor things in life and are too exhausted to face the major undertakings. There are times when we should reserve our own strength for the necessary things in life; this is, especially, when we should lean and depend on God. What does a boxer do in between the rounds of a boxing match? Rest, review strategies and refocus for the next round.

"THE MOST IMPORTANT THINGS YOU CAN HAVE FOR SUCCESS ARE…

1. YOUR HEALTH
2. YOUR EDUCATION (AND REGARD FOR OTHERS)
3. MOST IMPORTANTLY: YOUR LORD AND SAVIOR JESUS CHRIST" #14

We must keep our priorities in perspective. (This is a personal moral or ethical code to live by.)

Things that affect our well-being should always be protected. When we remain diligent about making rational choices, we will think; Will this disrupt my mental, emotional or spiritual health? Stay in school or on your job until you get what you went there for. Acquire your education but not at the expense of total disregard of others. Your education and freedom affect who you marry, where you live and your world view. Have faith in Jesus Christ; He will sustain you through life. Do everything for the Glory of God and not yourself. "Remember there are levels to acquiring faith.".. we must go through in order to come out victorious.

"TEAR YOUR TAIL WITH ME, IT WILL BE HARD MENDING IT" (Virginia Lanigan) #15

Forgiven doesn't mean forgotten.

My grandmother grew up in the south and she always talked about dealing with people with a long-handled spoon. After reviewing her life and the betrayals she endured, I could hardly believe there was any good in the world. But she spoke of learning from her mistakes and moving on. Langston Hughes said, "Life ain't been no crystal stair." When my grandmother was done (with a battle), she was done (with that person in general). You may be thinking, this shows unforgiveness. Look at it this way, you can forgive but it does not mean return to a degrading or hostile relationship.

“IF IT AIN’T THE MAIN EVENT IT’S JUST PRACTICE” #16

Try, try again.

We endeavor to make relationships work whether it be personal or professional but sometimes we must know when to let go. Donnie McClurkin said, “We fall down but we get up." Know that life will give you another chance, forgive yourself and move on. I know that sounds easier said than done when emotions are involved. The sun will rise again, and you will have another chance to make it right.

"WHAT DON'T COME OUT IN THE WASH, WILL COME OUT IN THE RINSE" #17

The truth will be revealed sooner or later.

Isn't it just like life to have cycles or seasons of revelation? You may not know the entire story of an incident but as time goes on it will be made known, especially if you seek the truth. Have you ever been falsely accused? Have you hoped that the facts will be made known? Just stand for what is right and in righteousness, God is our secret judge!

"YOU AIN'T GONNA MAKE ME CUSS" #18

Don't let them see you sweat.

I refuse to get upset. Joyce Meyers said it best: "The devil sets you up to get you upset!" Many people curse when they are at a loss for words and feel such frustration that all that is left in their vocabulary are four-letter words. "Death and life are in the power of the tongue," Proverbs 18:21 KJV. Similarly, James 3:3 teaches us, "When we put bits in the mouths of horses to make them obey us, we can turn the whole animal." NIV

“YOU’RE A FUNNY GIRL” #19

Choose happiness and bask in it.

My daughters have a great sense of humor. We laugh at each other's jokes and enjoy each other's company. Many families are not able to get along, show respect and treat each other with kindness. We go out of our way to support and show each other that we care. We try not to offend each other and rarely do.

“I GOT THE “CAN’T HELP ITS” #20

Empathy, love and compassion are alive and well in the world.

When we see each other struggling or in need, we offer help. We try not to loan money that we cannot just give. We are compelled by love to do for those we love and/or care about. When people know you need help and are not willing to help when they can, that is not love.

"FORGIVE YOURSELF AND DON'T DO IT AGAIN" #21

Forgiveness is for you.

Learn from your mistakes. That is why God put erasers on pencils to eliminate errors. Sometimes we are our worst critics. Consult with God, make plans, write it down, and you may choose to tell one person to help you be accountable. If you make an error, own it and move on. If you correct someone else, do it in love to help them improve rather than lecturing and putting them down.

No one likes a nag.

I once took a leadership class that taught us, when you tell a person one thing they did poorly, tell them 10 things they did well. This principle also applies to yourself. Never use profanity when correcting yourself and others. Sometimes we make an error, and we rehearse it over and over, but we must remember that the good things we do daily will not go unnoticed. Focus on the good you have done.

"A PIECE OF SHOE IS BETTER THAN NO SHOE" #22

Be grateful for what you do have.

Have you ever walked across hot pavement without shoes? Even a pair of flip-flops would be better than bare feet. Sometimes in life we feel like we are settling for less than what we want but sometimes it is necessary to work with where we are until we can achieve better. When dissatisfied with a job, it may be better to secure new employment, in advance, before departing. It would be better than leaving with no plan, especially when a family is involved. People may say there are no jobs, but it is not true. Maybe the job is not paying what a person thinks they deserve but they may not be searching for better employment while still working where they are. Is it pride that prevents a person from working a second job? Seek God's guidance. When a person has a bleeding injury the first aid treatment is to apply a bandage with direct pressure. If the bandage becomes soiled with blood apply additional dressing without removing the first bandage. Can you visualize your bills due and no source of income? Count the cost and ask God for direction. "When we plan God laughs". Do you remember the previous quote that said, "God is our provider!"

"IT PAYS TO READ" #23

Read the fine print. Pay attention to the details.

Everything we need to know has been written in a book somewhere. When our children learn to love to read early, it becomes the foundation for their educational future. If they see us read, they will try to mimic us as adults. A good reader has a future in the world.

“A LIE DOESN’T CARE WHO TELLS IT” #24

Lying and exaggerating the truth is not an art.

Practice telling the truth. If you tell one lie you will have to tell another to cover the first one. Then you must remember the lies so you can tell it again and again.

“YOU’RE THE SONS I NEVER HAD” #25

Don't be afraid to get your hands dirty.

My daughters have been my best companions in life, especially in their adult years. They had challenges in life, like most of us, to become the good and strong women they are. We now laugh at the immature deeds of their youth. Hopefully, this will encourage parents who think they will be so glad when their teenagers move out. It gets better but as you probably know, parenting is for life.

When I was raising my daughters, they wanted to have nice things. So, I tried to teach them the responsibilities and the life lessons that came along with having those privileges. Some of their tougher chores may have been reserved for boys but it taught them to be independent, hard-working and appreciative. Luke 12:48 says, "Everyone to whom much is given, of him much is required." ESV

“DON’T BE LIKE ME, BE BETTER THAN ME” #26

Allow your children to profit from your mistakes

Use my experiences to avoid errors in life. If we allow our children to grow into all that they can be, we must remain in the trenches of life to guide them. Many times, they rebel and say things like “I don’t want to do what you have chosen for me.” And you ask, "What do you want to do?” Surprisingly, they may say “I don’t know.” A friend of mine was guided by her father to go to medical school. He bought her a doctor kit as a child and later a chemistry set. She called him strict and old-fashioned. She later attended college still complaining of her father but stayed along the path he decided for her. In her third year of medical school, she decided her medical profession was a little more suited to her and became a doctor, nonetheless.

“I’VE BEEN WHERE YOU’RE TRYING TO GO” #27

I will share my experiences so you can avoid the pitfalls I have endured.

Usually this applies to a teenager. I would try to convince my daughters not to do something that would harm them. For example, my oldest granddaughter asked for assistance with a poem competition. We brainstormed together and came up with two appropriate poems. After deciding on the best one, she took the poem and showed it to her friend. The friend told her not to submit the one we chose. So, she decided to follow her friend’s advice. In the end, her friend won first place and my granddaughter won second place with the poem her friend had chosen. My granddaughter was upset because her friend changed her own poem to resemble the format of my granddaughter’s poem. In essence, one should follow the guidance of experience and wisdom.

"I CAN TALK TILL I'M BLUE IN THE FACE" #28

If you will not listen, I can save my breath.

We cannot make another human being do the right thing. We must instead find a way to reach them. Sometimes as parents we are so exhausted, we want to give up, but parenting is a life-time commitment. I do not claim to be an authority on everything but frequently we can see where things are headed way ahead of time.

"YOU PLAY WITH A PUPPY, HE'LL LICK YOUR MOUTH"
#29

Be careful of the company you keep.

"If the best, the smartest and brightest person you know is you, then change your associates." If you associate with negative people, it can change your positive outlook. Surround yourself with people that exemplify the character you are striving to attain. By the same token, no one is perfect and is subject to mistakes so do not make people your God.

“I KNOW I AM SOMEBODY BECAUSE GOD DON’T MAKE NO JUNK” #30

Believe in yourself.

When my daughters' were children I told them to affirm this quote. These are words that can encourage you as you learn who you are in life.

“STAY OUT OF GROWN FOLKS’ BUSINESS” #31

Stay in a child’s place.

When children chime-in on adult conversation...teach them manners and respect at an early age!

"I'VE NEVER SEEN THE RIGHTEOUS FORSAKEN OR THEIR SEED BEG FOR BREAD" #32

Psalms 37:25 reveals that God will meet your every need.

This Bible scripture is one of many that I have written out and placed on my bathroom mirror. It is one that has encouraged me after the death of my husband and entering the world of raising two daughters as a single mother (again). Who would have thought that I would have to face this challenge alone? But, I was never alone. Thank you, Lord, for sustaining me. I had a friend who has faced a similar crisis and she declared "I am going to have a nervous breakdown, I deserve one". Now, we laugh together at the thoughts we had during the storms of life. Be encouraged! God's got you.

“YESTERDAYS SCORE DOESN’T GO ON TODAYS’ BASEBALL GAME” #33

Focus on the future.

Everyday has its own challenges. Do not look backward trying to go forward. Tyler Perry said it best: “I know why a rear-view mirror is smaller than a windshield." The best you do today will not fill-up tomorrow's deeds. Encourage yourself, dust yourself off and keep moving. You are not the only one. If success were easy everyone would have it. Never give up!

“BITTER WATER AND SWEET WATER DON’T RUN DOWN THE SAME RIVER” #34

Life and death are in the power of the tongue.

If we do not control our tongue, how will we succeed? How can we choose to curse and praise with the same mouth? Many people use foul language out of frustration and anger “For what you say flows from what is in your heart,” Luke 6:45 NLT

"ENOUGH SAID" #35

We have got the picture (you can stop talking).

Sometimes less is more. No one likes to be nagged or lectured, so try to keep your message short and sweet.

"CAN'T STOP WON'T STOP ...GOT TO MAKE ITMAKE IT" #36

Encourage yourself to keep moving forward.

Some military training camps have recruits to recite these words during physical training. But it can apply to any difficult task when you want to give up. If success were easy everyone would have it. We talk about the American dream and the land of opportunity, but no one said it would be easy. Many have advantages but those of us from humble beginnings must strive long and hard despite the odds. Do not lose sight of the goal. Surround yourself with true believers and continue to put one foot ahead of the other until you reach your destination. Then, reach back and help someone else.

"DON'T SWEAT THE SMALL STUFF" #37

Relax, trust God!

Where can we go that God cannot order our steps? "Be anxious for nothing" but choose your battles. It is rarely as bad as we imagine. Nothing is a matter of life and death except life and death. The sun and Son will rise again.

"A WATCHED POT NEVER BOILS" #38

Be patient, it will work out for you.

Literally and figuratively, if you stand at the stove in anticipation of water coming to a boil, it seems to take forever. But occupy yourself and prepare to maintain a conscious eye on your surroundings. Settle down and know that God has everything under control. Again, be anxious for nothing.

“IF IT AIN’T THE POT CALLING THE KETTLE BLACK” #39

"Let him who is without sin among you, be the first to throw a stone..." -John 8:7 ESV

Some people like to point fingers at a person's faults even though they have been guilty of the same thing. Generally, when a person tells their perception of what you did it's usually through the scope of what they would have done given the same circumstance.

“I WAS HERE WHEN YOU GOT HERE” #40

There's nothing new under the sun.

Many times, children think they know just as much as their parents. Should I tell them or let them guess? It is amusing when they finally discover just how little they know. The more I learn, the more I discover how much I do not know. “I taught you everything you know but not everything that I know." Sometimes when developing relationships or friendships people can get too comfortable and forget about boundaries. They may forget that they have been welcomed into the family “by invitation” not by birth-right.

“BULLETS DON'T HAVE NAMES ON THEM” #41

Be aware, stay alert.

If a crowd is gathered in the street and bullets are shot and innocent people stand by, anyone can be hit.

When teenagers or even adults decide to hang-out in the street just because, remember danger is everywhere…children have even been shot by stray bullets that have been shot through their homes while sleeping in bed. #AllLivesMatter.

“IF THEY DON’T SHOW IT, THEY DON’T HAVE IT” #42

Love is an action word.

When examining the components of love expression, many people explain I am just not an emotional person; I cannot show affection. When you see a friend in need and you have the ability to assist them but refuse to, is it out of selfishness or a lack of love? Some say, “I got my success by putting in hard work and you can get yours the best way you can. You’re on your own. I’m not your leaning post or the welfare office.” Some people call this tough love when they're trying to teach a person to stand on their own two feet.

"YOU'RE DO TO SUIT YOURSELF, BUT IF IT WAS ME..." #43

Allow others to make choices.

There are times when we recognize friends or family in a crisis, and they choose to remain in a destructive or toxic relationship. Although this is not the path that you would choose for them, they have the right to make their own decisions.

“WELCOME” #44
Welcome to adulthood

There tends to always be a young person who wants to be 21-years-old so they can do whatever they want. Unfortunately, most do not wait until they are 21 as it seems to be more fun if they sneak and do something underage. When one steps into adulthood and all its responsibilities, there is no turning back. This “welcome” expression parallels with, “so you wanted to be grown, this is what grown folks do”. If you choose to return to childhood after attaining the ripe old age of 21, by court order, someone else will be appointed as your guardian and they will make all your decisions for you. Sorry, that is the way it is. So, I remind my grandchildren to stay young and innocent, if possible. My oldest granddaughter frequently approaches or calls me from college and in a small baby voice says,” Grand-nana, I was just thinking…". This is usually a sure sign that she has encountered a new experience in adulthood.

"WE'VE GOT TO LIVE WHEN THIS IS OVER" #45

Spending should be done in moderation

This phrase usually applies to overextending, whether it is time, money or energy. Sometimes when we are forced to budget, we bump into the walls of the budget to buy one more thing, whether needed or not. But we have got to plan and stick to it. Some adults and teens alike have not arrived at the discipline it takes in association with spending and budgeting. This same discipline is associated with time management. If we are indulging in a fun activity and you know you need to go to work or school the next day, it can be challenging to pull away and give our bodies a chance to rest. My family laughs when I go to sleep at 5:00 PM because my alarm is set to wake me up at 3:30 AM for work. However, it is one thing to work when you are tired, and it is another to have several days of exhaustion. The hardest discipline is self-discipline. Do you remember the story of Cinderella? She had a reason for leaving the ball early. Some peoples' attitude is, you can sleep when you are "dead" but that is not a practical or healthy way of living.

"GET MAD AND STAY MAD" #46

Keep that same energy.

The word "mad" is the level of emotion sometimes necessary to stay motivated after failing to reach a goal. How easily we forget the disappointment associated with working hard to succeed. A certain amount of energy is needed to be maintained to persevere. One of my greatest sources of energy is fear of failure. I feel like an avalanche is following me down a snow drift when I am running toward a goal and I do not look back for fear of being distracted. It never fails in a horror movie, for someone to run in the woods away from a monster and start to look back, lose their footing and fall. That is me, don't look back, just keep running!

"FOCUS PANDA" #47

Keep your eyes on the prize.

Kung Fu Panda is one of my favorite and most inspirational movies. Some writers try to get a message across but choose to put it in a form of entertainment for children. I am a "nugget finder" looking for nuggets of wisdom in every scenario. This movie gives me a lot of insight about how appearances are judged. Do not be afraid to step out of your comfort zone, even if others do not believe in you or think you are the chosen one. That is God's decision. Most times, we want to surround ourselves with "positive knowing thoughts of love" but, when that is not possible either change your association or keep your ideas safe, until you are in the presence of like-minds.

“IS THERE AN ECHO IN HERE” #48

You heard me right.

When a person wants you to repeat what you've said but you are sure they heard you the first time, we may ask, “Is there an echo in here?” Other times when someone is trying to deflect from answering a question, they may respond by repeating you: “Where have you been?” and they say, “Where have I been?” If you have ever experienced this, it is a form of “selective” hearing loss. Many spouses also exhibit this when it is something they do not want to hear or do. In fact, they will repeat what you said and smile.

“THERE’S A DEAD CAT ON THE LINE” #49

Something isn't quite right.

This statement may involve 2 true statements and a lie. Whenever you hear information from a person and something just doesn't add up, you may feel free to interject this phrase. For instance, if it does not quite gel, it is probably because it is not entirely true. It is quite interesting when a person repeats something they heard and want you to analyze it for them but in the back of your mind you wonder what part of the story is fabricated?

"WHEN YOU DON'T HAVE LOVE, ALL YOU HAVE IS THE LAW" #50

"What's love got to do with it?"

When couples, families or even businesses decide they can no longer operate in love, the law will decide what they should do. So many people chose to argue, fight or seek to destroy the one they once loved. They want the other person to hurt as much as they hurt. Some even say, "If I can't have you no one will" and they actively set-out to ruin their loved-one's life. When there are children involved, they may be forced to choose sides. Let me tell you, the legal system will objectively decide what you should do. If you want to survive this situation, take your feelings out of the middle of this and follow the letter of the law. If there is child visitation or some other division of personal items, let the law guide you even if you do not like the outcome. I have been in this situation and I asked God to take my feelings out of the middle of the situation so that I could live again. Over time, I healed and was able to move on with my life. Additionally, the less you talk about it with multiple people, the better off you will be. You can get more things. What is money if you do not have peace of mind. Be encouraged! "This too shall pass."

"CLICK, CLICK"
(Testimony 1)

A letter arrived in the mail with what I thought was the worst news I would ever face. I took the letter to church and after worship service brought it to my (then) Pastors Curtis and Ann. I took the letter from the envelope and placed it under the scarf that draped across the communion table. We prayed over the letter and I went home, leaving the letter at the altar. The next day at work I shared my sadness with my friend. She asked where the letter was and I told her I only had the envelope. She asked if I wanted her and her husband to pray with me. I said, "Yes." She took the envelope and gave it to her husband who was a two-time liver transplant recipient. He placed the envelope on his head and covered it with his baseball cap. For 3 days we prayed. On the third day, I was standing in the bathroom preparing for work. As I stood brushing my teeth and looking in the mirror, I heard the voice of the Lord say, "Call the bank." I knew it was not payday, so I hesitated. While standing there looking in the mirror I saw a cloud appear over the bathtub behind me. I did not turn around. A muscular arm came from the cloud and with the palm facing down. My house appeared in the hand with the roof in the palm area and the fingers of the hand extending around the sides of the house. The hand lifted the house, and I could hear an audible “click, click,” like a Rubik’s cube. The hand repositioned the house, placed it down and was drawn back up into the cloud and disappeared. I just stood there looking through the mirror at the spot where the cloud had vanished.

After a few minutes I walked into the bedroom and called the bank. As they automatic teller announced the account balance, I pressed #1 again as it repeated the thousands and thousands of dollars that had been deposited that morning. Someone on the other side of the country had pressed "send" and the funds were deposited into my account. I needed an interpretation for what I had just experienced. My pastor announced that my house was not just the structure where I lived, but rather my household was covered by the hand of God. This included my children and the rest of the family, my health, my spiritual life, finance, social, education and all my concerns were in the hand of God. I know this is true, as years have passed since that day and what I have faced since then have made that problem appear as a “small fry on a value menu." God has kept me through so many crises that I can look back and recall what He has already brought me through.

The cover photograph of this book is of the house I was living in when I saw the hand of God pick up my home and place it on a firm foundation. About three months after the vision of the house experience, a woman arrived at my home with this photo. She worked for an aerial view photography company and offered to sell this picture to me. She said, "We took an aerial photograph of your house…we want you to see what God sees when He looks down on your home from Heaven."

“YOU’VE GOT TO GET YOUR FEET WET”
(Testimony 2)

When I applied to graduate school I prayed for guidance and acceptance into the program. I had a dream that I was on a double Ferris Wheel. While I was riding to the top wheel, the ride rotated and the seat where I was sitting was suddenly at the bottom of the ride. As the wheel turned my feet were hanging down and I was wearing new white gym shoes. It had been raining and my feet passed through the muddy water below. I awoke and the voice of the Lord said, “You’ve got to get your feet wet."

The water under the Ferris Wheel was muddy, which let me know that the application process was not going to be clear-cut. I would need to step out of my comfort zone and apply to programs outside of my home state. I applied nationwide and was accepted into multiple state programs.

“YOUR NAME IS SARAH AND I KNOW WHAT I PROMISED YOU” (Testimony 3)

I had applied for employment in Alabama but did not get the job. I was extremely disappointed and prayed to God asking, why and what was His plan for me? I know if it is not the "main event" then it is just practice. Still, I felt disappointed and wanted to understand. During the night I was returning to bed from the bathroom, and I heard the voice of God and He said “Vanessa, your name is Sarah and I know what I promised you (pause) and I don’t need your help.” I remembered the Biblical story of Sarah, the wife of Abraham. God had made a promise to her, but she was not patient enough to wait for God to fulfill His promise. She decided to help fulfill the promise of God by having her husband lay with her maidservant, Hagar. The promise belonged to Sarah and it was not her place to take matters into her own hands. I thank God for revealing His promise to me and reminding me that He does not need my help.

FAREWELL

Hopefully, the contents of this book have been informative as well as entertaining. Many times, I smiled as my fingers typed these words and could tell that some readers will find it full of wisdom and humor. I deliberately tried to remain focused on topics that may be of interest to you or have been discussed by our family and embraced as a part of our lifestyle. Although we speak proper grammar, sometimes situations are beyond the scope of our vocabulary, so we resort to certain words that express our feelings best. My mother, grandmother, friends and extended family have contributed to this collection of thoughts and phrases. Other times I have been inspired by a poem, song or words spoken. As we work toward our destiny and become more enlightened, we become a product of everything we have ever experienced, whether good or bad, while choosing to welcome certain experiences and discard others. Nevertheless, I thank God for everything He has brought me through. I feel that I have so much to share I cannot tell it all. So, in my next book I will continue to share, inspire, and make others a part of our reading family.

In lasting thought, I thank God for the precious grandchildren

He has blessed me with:

Farenscia

Aiden

Makenzie

Adele

Makenna